DREAMWORKS

KUNG FU PANDA

Walter Foster
Jr.

Step-by-step illustrations by Joe Vance.

Published by Walter Foster Jr.,
an imprint of Quarto Publishing Group USA Inc.
6 Orchard Road, Suite 100, Lake Forest, CA 92630
Printed in China
3 5 7 9 10 8 6 4 2

FSC
www.fsc.org
MIX
Paper from
responsible sources
FSC® C101537

TABLE OF CONTENTS

TOOLS & MATERIALS

You'll need to gather a few simple drawing tools before you begin. Start with a drawing pencil and eraser so you can easily erase any mistakes. Make sure you have a sharpener and ruler too. To add color to your drawings, use markers, colored pencils, crayons, or even acrylic or watercolor paint.

drawing pencil
and paper

eraser

sharpener

colored pencils

felt-tip
markers

paintbrush
and paints

HOW TO USE THIS BOOK

You can draw any of the characters in this book by following these simple steps.

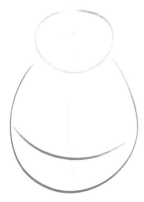

Start your drawing in the middle of the paper so you won't run out of room.

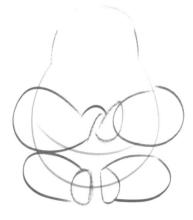

Each new step appears in blue, so you'll always know what to draw next.

Take your time and copy the blue lines.

Refine the lines of your drawing. Then add the details.

Darken the lines you want to keep and erase the rest.

Add color to your drawing with colored pencils, markers, paints, or crayons!

SIZE CHART

Mantis   Bao   Shifu   Mr. Ping   Monkey   Viper   Crane   Mei Mei

Tigress   Po   Li   Kai

THE FURIOUS FIVE

Throughout their many adventures together, the Furious Five have taken on more evil forces and challenging battles than they can count, proving that they are a powerful force to be reckoned with time and time again. Dragon Warrior Po and Masters Tigress, Monkey, Crane, Mantis, and Viper have distinct kung fu fighting styles that make each member a unique and irreplaceable part of the team.

PO'S FIGHTING STYLE

* Nontraditional, innovative, unique, authentic
* Strategy: Exploits physical attributes as a 6-foot-2, 260-pound panda (including his belly and rear end!)
* Signature strength: Utilizes perceived weaknesses as his greatest assets

TIGRESS' FIGHTING STYLE

* Powerful, strong, firm, aggressive, agile, elegant, honorable
* Strategy: Strikes directly without hesitation; stays close to the ground
* Signature strength: Acrobatic moves that are effective, yet honorable—never using her claws

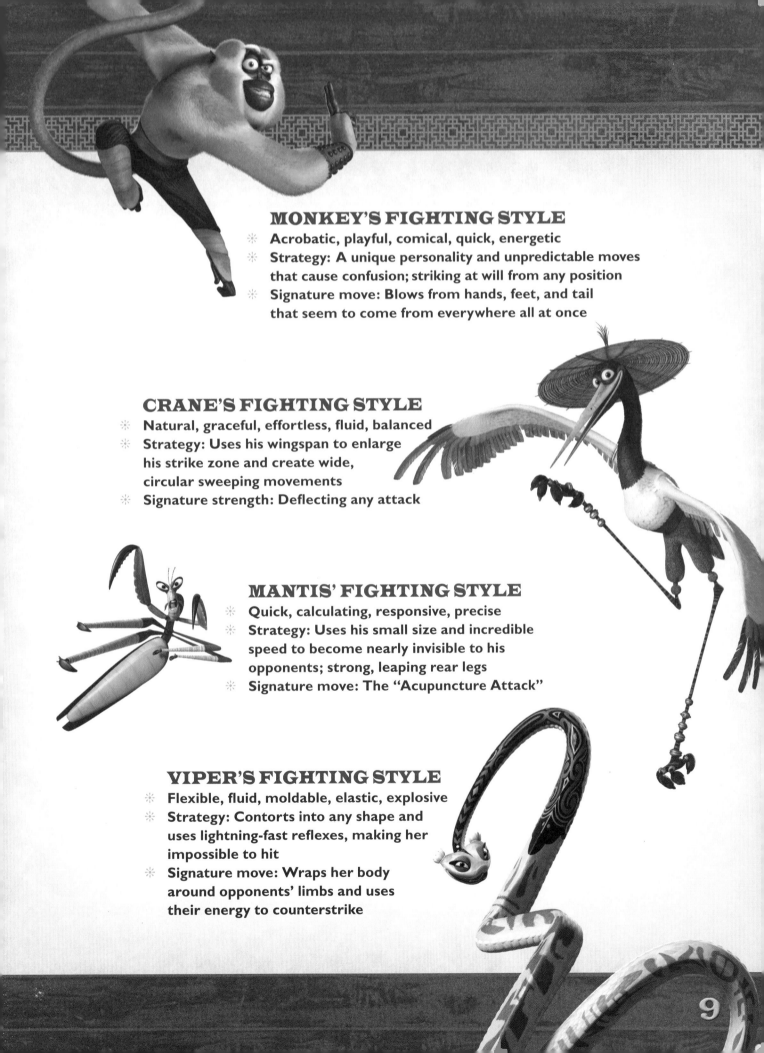

MONKEY'S FIGHTING STYLE

* Acrobatic, playful, comical, quick, energetic
* Strategy: A unique personality and unpredictable moves that cause confusion; striking at will from any position
* Signature move: Blows from hands, feet, and tail that seem to come from everywhere all at once

CRANE'S FIGHTING STYLE

* Natural, graceful, effortless, fluid, balanced
* Strategy: Uses his wingspan to enlarge his strike zone and create wide, circular sweeping movements
* Signature strength: Deflecting any attack

MANTIS' FIGHTING STYLE

* Quick, calculating, responsive, precise
* Strategy: Uses his small size and incredible speed to become nearly invisible to his opponents; strong, leaping rear legs
* Signature move: The "Acupuncture Attack"

VIPER'S FIGHTING STYLE

* Flexible, fluid, moldable, elastic, explosive
* Strategy: Contorts into any shape and uses lightning-fast reflexes, making her impossible to hit
* Signature move: Wraps her body around opponents' limbs and uses their energy to counterstrike

THE STORY OF KUNG FU PANDA 3

In *Kung Fu Panda 3,* Po continues his now legendary adventures of awesomeness and must face two hugely epic, but very different threats. Po has saved China countless times, but none of that has prepared him for his greatest challenge yet—teaching kung fu! In the latest story of *Kung Fu Panda,* Po reunites with his biological father, Li, and returns home to the secret Panda Village (much to the chagrin of his goose dad, Mr. Ping, who tags along to keep an eye on his boy). At the village, Po meets other pandas for the first time and learns what it's like to be a real panda. But when Po realizes the world is in danger from Kai, an ancient evil spirit who is bent on wiping out kung fu, it is up to him to train the cuddly, clumsy pandas to prepare for an epic kung fu throw down.

PO

After years of dreaming of fighting alongside the Furious Five, the greatest kung fu warriors in China, Po, an apprentice at his father's noodle shop, is fatefully chosen as the new Dragon Warrior. Though this panda's training style appears to be more about dumplings than discipline, Po's tenacious spirit and unique approach to kung fu help him defeat even the most masterful villains. Despite all of the fame, Po is the same humble, fanboy panda. Though he's living out his dream fighting alongside the Furious Five, Po's journey is not complete. The Dragon Warrior must face new challenges and responsibilities on his way to becoming the best he can be.

1

6

1

6

SHIFU

Wise Master Shifu is the trainer of China's greatest kung fu warriors. He's a strict, disciplined teacher who pushes his students to achieve their greatest potential. Though small, Shifu is a powerhouse, exerting maximum force with minimal effort, exemplified by his signature move, the Wuxi Finger Hold, with which he is capable of overpowering even the strongest opponent. Shifu's skills border on the mystical—he often appears where he's least expected, seemingly within the blink of an eye.

1

MR. PING

Mr. Ping may have lost his best (and only) employee to kung fu greatness, but he couldn't be more proud of his adopted panda son. In fact, Mr. Ping has decked out the noodle shop in honor of Po's epic exploits. But like any father who watches his child grow up and have a life of his own, Mr. Ping worries about being forgotten. He coddles his number one (and only) son, making sure to always have extra helpings of bean buns, dumplings, and noodle soup ready to feed the Dragon Warrior whenever he stops by. Mr. Ping loves three things more than anything in the world: Po, noodles, and selling noodles.

1

4

5

TIGRESS

Master Tigress is the strongest and boldest member of the Furious Five. Basically she's everything you'd want in a hero: overachieving, brave, and fearless. She'd do anything to save the day. She's unwaveringly loyal to Po and what he represents as the Dragon Warrior. But underneath her stoic, iron-jawed (and iron-hand, iron-feet, pretty much iron-everything) exterior is a warm compassion that others seldom see.

4

5

6

MONKEY

Mischievous, playful, and enthusiastic, Master Monkey likes a good joke, but his easygoing attitude masks cunning martial arts ability. More street-smart than the rest of the Furious Five, Monkey is an unpredictable prankster who is as fierce as he is clever and funny. While he likes to goof off as much as Po, in a fight Monkey's the guy you can count on to always have your back.

1

CRANE

Master Crane is the pragmatist of the group. Reluctant to resort to violence, he's a "think first, punch second" kind of bird. Sometimes a well-placed quip is the strongest technique. He'll try to avoid a fight if at all possible, but if he can't, he'll do everything he can to win. The safety of his fellow Furious Five is his first priority. He's willing to risk his life to protect them.

1

6

MANTIS

Master Mantis may be the smallest of the Five, but that doesn't mean he can't subdue even the largest opponents. The little guy has a textbook Napoleon complex: strong, fast, and tiny, he possesses a quick temper and is ready to "throw down" at the slightest insult.

1

VIPER

Master Viper is the "mother hen" of the group. It takes a cool head and a warm heart to manage the sometimes conflicting personalities of the Furious Five. But don't let her gentle nature fool you. Viper is a lightning-fast warrior capable of taking down the most intimidating foe. Her power lies in her strength, her sinuous nature, her precision . . . oh, and then there's that deadly strike of hers.

1

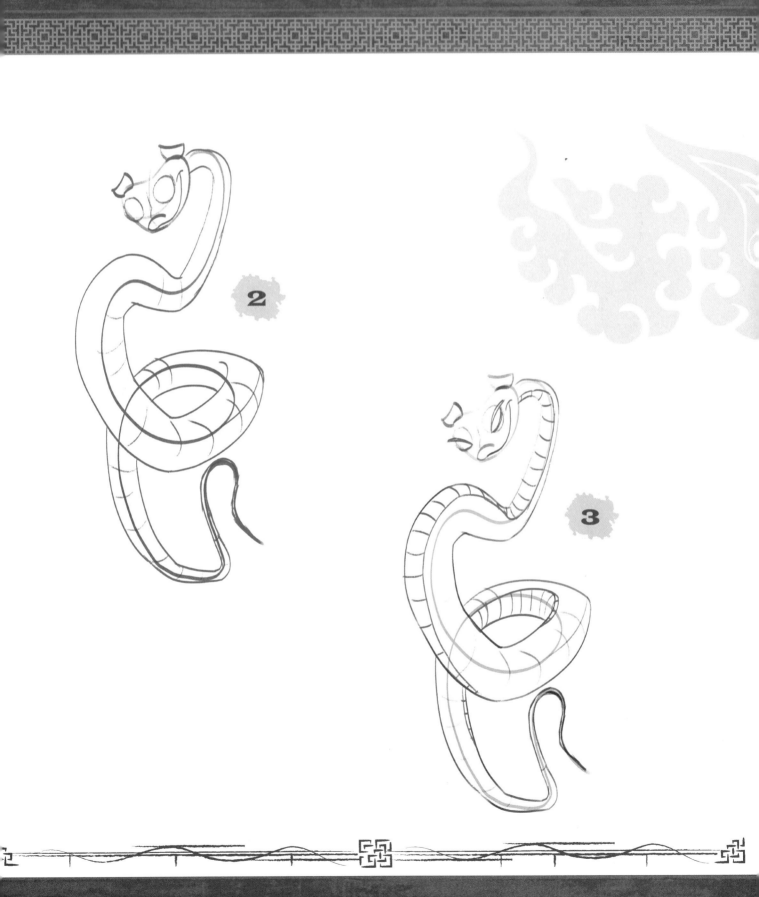

2

3

LI

Imagine who Po would be without the discipline of kung fu—and that's Li. Po's panda dad is an exuberant, fun-loving panda always up for a good time, whether that's eating and napping, or napping and eating, and maybe even hot-tubbing too! But underneath that warm smile and engaging laugh, he's been nursing a broken heart for the family he lost years ago. Believing his beloved son was lost to him forever, Li learns that Po is alive and sets out to bring him home. But his arrival in the Valley of Peace is complicated by the fact that Po already has an adventurous life as the famed Dragon Warrior, as well as an adopted goose dad, Mr. Ping, who won't like being replaced.

1

BAO

Are you curious about Bao? Well he's more curious about you. What's your name? How old are you? Where are you from? Why are you from there? What are you? Are you a panda? You don't look like a panda. How come you're not a panda? This cute little fluff ball is a bottomless pit of panda inquisitiveness. Whip-smart, he'll poke a hole in any story that smells fishy to him. When Po and Mr. Ping arrive in the Panda Village, they are immediately subjected to his adorable brand of scrutiny. Bao helps teach Po the panda way of life, and when danger threatens the village, Po teaches Bao to become the best panda he can be.

1

6

MEI MEI

Mei Mei is the most confident panda in the Panda Village and the best ribbon dancer by a long shot. (It totally doesn't matter that there are no other ribbon dancers in the village. If there were, she'd **STILL** be the best. Cuz she's awesome.) Most pandas in the Panda Village live easygoing, laid-back lives filled with sleeping, eating, napping, snacking, sleep-snacking, and nap-eating. But Mei Mei is the opposite. She's extremely motivated, her standards are extremely high, and nothing impresses her. (Well, nothing except her. Cuz she's awesome.) When Po arrives in the Panda Village and comes face to face with a female panda for the first time, Mei Mei isn't surprised that his mind is blown. (See above re: awesome.) But in the end, Po does earn her respect when he helps her discover something new about herself. And that discovery involves nunchucks and some amazing kung fu.

1

6

KAI

Centuries ago, Kai and Oogway were fearsome warriors, brothers-in-arms who fought side by side in countless battles. There was great harmony between them until one day, they discovered *chi*—the life energy that flows through all things. Kai, ever hungry for more power, wanted to keep it for himself and found a way to take chi from others. Brothers became enemies and in an earth-shaking battle, Oogway defeated Kai and banished him to the Spirit Realm for all eternity. During his centuries in the Spirit Realm, Kai's hatred and resentment has festered and grown. When he defeats Oogway in the Spirit Realm and returns to earth, Kai is desperate to obliterate Oogway's legacy—his precious kung fu. Kai's insatiable appetite for power and revenge ultimately leads him to a confrontation with Oogway's greatest student—Po, the Dragon Warrior.

1

6